DISCOVERING THE UNITED STATES

Arizona

BY IB LARSEN

An Imprint of Abdo Publishing
abdobooks.com

abdobooks.com

Published by Abdo Publishing, a division of ABDO, PO Box 398166, Minneapolis, Minnesota 55439.

Printed in China.
052024
092024

THIS BOOK CONTAINS RECYCLED MATERIALS

Cover Photo: Zack Frank/Shutterstock Images
Interior Photos: Shutterstock Images, 4–5, 9 (top right), 14 (bottom), 18, 22, 25, 26, 28 (top right), 28 (bottom); Kit Leong/Shutterstock Images, 6; John D. Sirlin/Shutterstock Images, 9 (top left); Raeann Davies/Shutterstock Images, 9 (bottom left); Pamela Au/Shutterstock Images, 9 (bottom right); Kenneth Keifer/Shutterstock Images, 10; David Ryan/Alamy, 12–13; Filip Bjorkman/Shutterstock Images, 14 (top); Brent Hofacker/Shutterstock Images, 16; Kevin Ruck/Shutterstock Images, 20–21; Red Line Editorial, 28 (top left), 29

Editor: Haley Williams
Series Designer: Katharine Hale

Library of Congress Control Number: 2023949215

Publisher's Cataloging-in-Publication Data

Names: Larsen, Ib, author.
Title: Arizona / by Ib Larsen
Description: Minneapolis, Minnesota: Abdo Publishing, 2025 | Series: Discovering the United States | Includes online resources and index.
Identifiers: ISBN 9781098293734 (lib. bdg.) | ISBN 9798384913009 (ebook)
Subjects: LCSH: U.S. states--Juvenile literature. | Arizona--History--Juvenile literature. | Southwestern States--Juvenile literature. | Physical geography--United States--Juvenile literature.
Classification: DDC 973--dc23

All population data taken from:
"Estimates of Population by Sex, Race, and Hispanic Origin: April 1, 2020 to July 1, 2022." *US Census Bureau, Population Division*, June 2023, census.gov.

CONTENTS

Over time, natural processes have caused the Meteor Crater to become less deep. Today, it is around 550 feet (168 m) deep.

CHAPTER 1

The Meteor Crater

About 50,000 years ago, a **meteorite** around 100 to 165 feet (30–50 m) wide hit Earth. It struck the planet with great force. The impact made a crater about 4,000 feet (1,200 m) wide and 700 feet (210 m) deep.

The Barringer Space Museum features a space capsule from the 1960s. The capsule was used to train astronauts before they went to the moon.

Today, this crater lies in the middle of a desert in the state of Arizona. It is known as the Meteor Crater or the Barringer Meteorite Crater. It was named after scientist Daniel Barringer. He studied the area in the early 1900s. Visitors can take a tour around the crater's edge. They can also visit the nearby Barringer Space Museum to learn about meteorite impacts. Visiting the Meteor Crater is one of the many fun things to do in Arizona.

Arizona's Land

Arizona is in the West region of the United States. California and Nevada border it to the east. The northwestern corner meets Utah, Colorado, and New Mexico at a single point.

This point is known as the Four Corners Monument. The country of Mexico borders Arizona in the south.

Arizona is home to several deserts. The Sonoran Desert is in the southwestern part of the state. It is one of the hottest deserts in the world. Arizona shares the Mojave Desert with Nevada, California, and Utah. The Colorado Plateau in the north also has some desert land.

The Summer Monsoon

In July, **humid** air from the Pacific Ocean arrives in Arizona. It causes a lot of rain to fall in the state over the next several months. This is usually the wettest time of the year. People in Arizona refer to this period as the summer monsoon.

Arizona Facts

DATE OF STATEHOOD
February 14, 1912

CAPITAL
Phoenix

POPULATION
7,359,197

AREA
113,990 square miles
(295,233 sq km)

STATE BIRD

Cactus wren

STATE TREE

Palo verde

STATE FLOWER

Saguaro cactus blossoms

STATE BUTTERFLY

Two-tailed swallowtail

Each US state has a different population, size, and capital city. States also have state symbols.

However, not all of Arizona is desert. There are some forests and grasslands as well. Most of Arizona's forestland is found in the central and southeastern parts of the state.

The climate in southern Arizona is mainly dry. This region usually receives little to no rain.

Arizona's Climate

Arizona's climate varies because of **elevation**. Areas at higher elevations have milder summers. They also receive more rain and snow. Some of Arizona's deserts can get very hot. Temperatures can reach up to 128 degrees Fahrenheit (53°C). The state capital, Phoenix, also gets very hot in the summer.

Further Evidence

Look at the website below. Does it give any new evidence to support Chapter One?

Arizona

abdocorelibrary.com/discovering-arizona

Although the Hohokam culture no longer exists, experts say the Pima people in southern Arizona are descendants of the Hohokam.

The People of Arizona

The first people came to Arizona around 13,500 years ago. They are known as the Clovis and Folsom peoples. Over time, new cultures appeared. One was the Hohokam people. They dug huge waterways to **irrigate** their crops.

The Spanish were some of the first European settlers to arrive in Arizona. The yellow and red from Spain's flag, *bottom*, are used in Arizona's state flag.

Today, there are 22 federally recognized American Indian nations in Arizona. The largest include the Navajo Nation and the Apache. More than 5 percent of people in Arizona were American Indians in 2022.

Early settlers of Arizona came from the eastern United States in the 1870s. They were searching for silver and copper. Since the 1900s, the Hispanic population of Arizona has grown. Many people came from Mexico or have Mexican **heritage**.

In 2022, almost 33 percent of Arizona's population was Hispanic or Latino. About 53 percent were white, and 6 percent were Black. Asian people made up 4 percent of the population.

Many people enjoy putting taco toppings on their fry bread. Others put powdered sugar or honey on top.

Culture

Fry bread is an American Indian dish enjoyed by many people in Arizona. It is made by frying dough in oil. The dish is said to have originated during an event known as the Long Walk. This event took place in 1864. The US government moved more than 10,000 Diné (Navajo) people to a reservation far from their home.

The chimichanga is another popular dish in Arizona. It first became popular in the city of Tucson. The dish is made by deep-frying a burrito.

The Long Walk

Hundreds of Diné people died during the Long Walk. Thousands more died of illness and hunger once they arrived at the Bosque Redondo Indian Reservation in New Mexico. In 1868, the US government allowed the Diné people to return to parts of their homeland in Arizona.

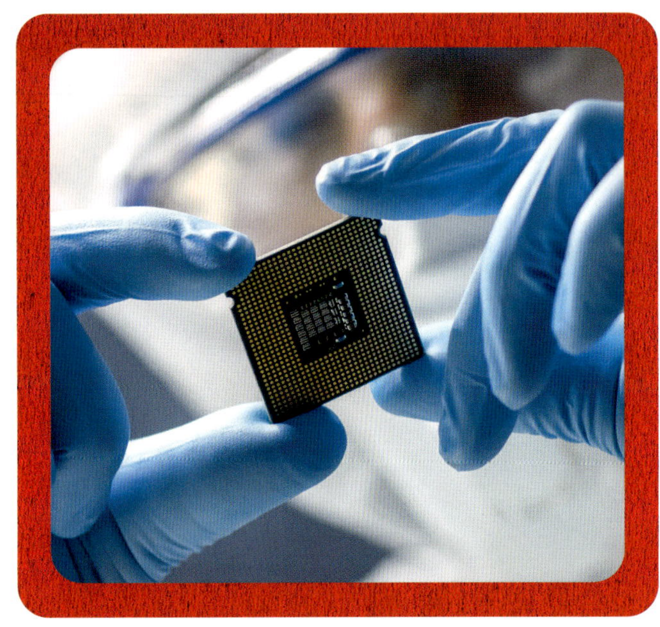

Intel and Microchip Technology are a few of the many companies in Arizona known for making parts for electronic devices.

Industry

Many people in Arizona have **manufacturing** jobs in factories. They make electronics and metal products. Some areas in Arizona have good soil for planting crops. Farmers plant cotton and lettuce in those areas. Other farmers raise cattle and pigs. Many people have jobs in the health-care industry as well. These include people who are nurses and doctors.

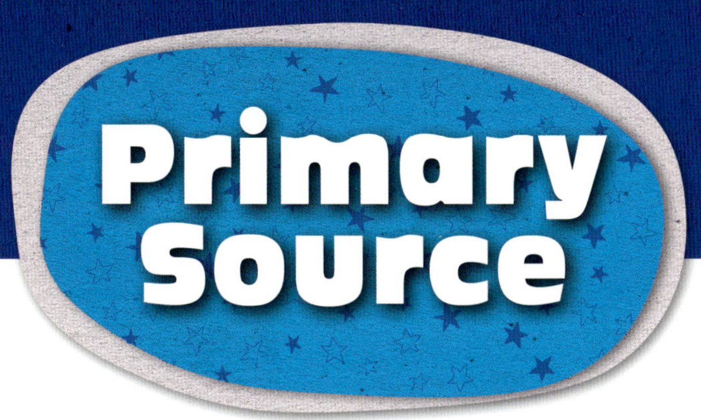

Reed Johnson, regional manager of an Arizona restaurant chain, described why people love the chimichanga:

> It's a combination of flavors. There's a little bit for everybody. . . . It's a great-looking dish. It looks appetizing. People eat with their eyes as well as their mouths.

Source: John Henderson, "Who Fried the Burrito First?" *Mercury News*, 10 Feb. 2007, mercurynews.com. Accessed 25 Sept. 2023.

What's the Big Idea?

Read this quote carefully. What is its main idea? Explain how the main idea is supported by details.

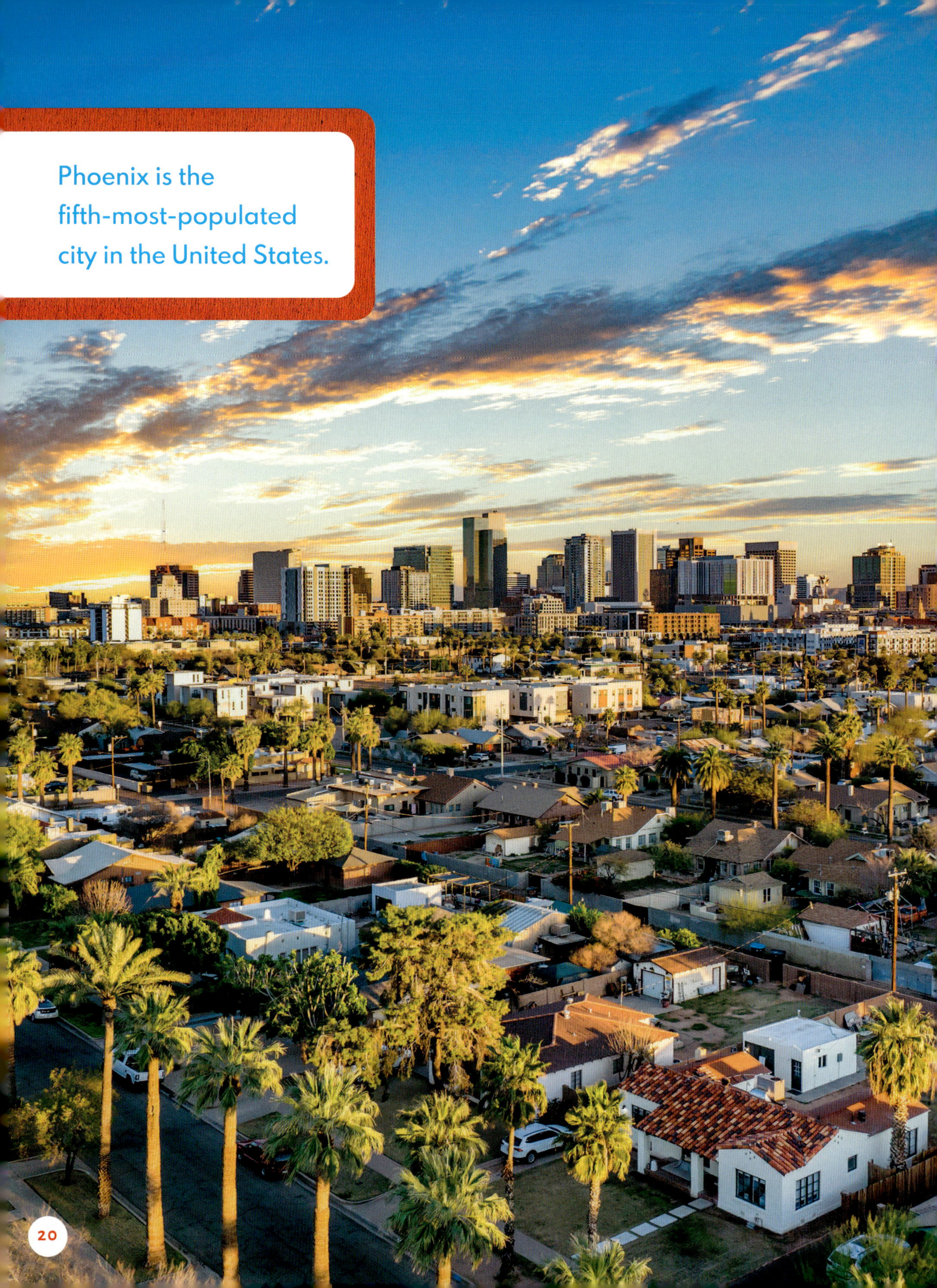

Phoenix is the fifth-most-populated city in the United States.

CHAPTER 3

Places in Arizona

The state capital, Phoenix, is Arizona's largest city. The next three largest cities are Tucson, Mesa, and Chandler. There are many things to see and do in Arizona's towns and cities.

In Phoenix, people can visit the Musical Instruments Museum.

In 2022, around 4.7 million people visited the Grand Canyon.

It has a huge collection of musical instruments for visitors to learn about. People visiting Tucson can see lots of animals at the Reid Park Zoo. And the Superstition Wilderness Area in Mesa is a popular place to go hiking and fishing.

Parks

Arizona is home to Grand Canyon National Park. It is one of the most famous national parks in the United States. The Grand Canyon officially became a national park in 1919. Today, visitors can tour the canyon's edge or hike through the canyon. They can also ride rafts down the Colorado River.

The Grand Canyon

The deepest point of the Grand Canyon is more than 1 mile (1.6 km) below its edge. Over the course of 6 million years, the Colorado River carved the canyon into what it is today. The layers of rock in the canyon are different shades of red, yellow, and green.

There are two other national parks in Arizona. Petrified Forest National Park is named after the many tree **fossils** found there. Saguaro National Park lets visitors hike through patches of saguaro cacti. These are the largest cacti in the United States.

Landmarks

Arizona has several notable landmarks. The Hoover Dam was the tallest dam in the world when it was completed in 1935. It spans the Colorado River between Arizona and Nevada's border. Water from the dam is used in different ways across the southwestern United States. The dam also creates electricity. This power is used in parts of California, Nevada, and Arizona.

Havasu Falls is one of five waterfalls in the Havasupai Indian Reservation.

People can also visit the Havasu Falls at the Havasupai Indian Reservation. The waterfall is known for its blue-green water. Visitors hike 10 miles (16 km) on a trail to get to the waterfall.

There are many beautiful sights to see in the state of Arizona.

Arizona has many other interesting landmarks. It also has a fascinating history and beautiful cultures. Visitors can look over the edge of the Grand Canyon. They can learn about the plants and animals that live in the state. Or they can explore important historical sites. Everybody who visits the state of Arizona can find something fun to do.

Explore Online

Visit the website below. Does it give any new information about the Hoover Dam that wasn't in Chapter Three?

Hoover Dam

abdocorelibrary.com/discovering-arizona

State Map

KEY

 Capital

 Park

 City or town

Point of interest

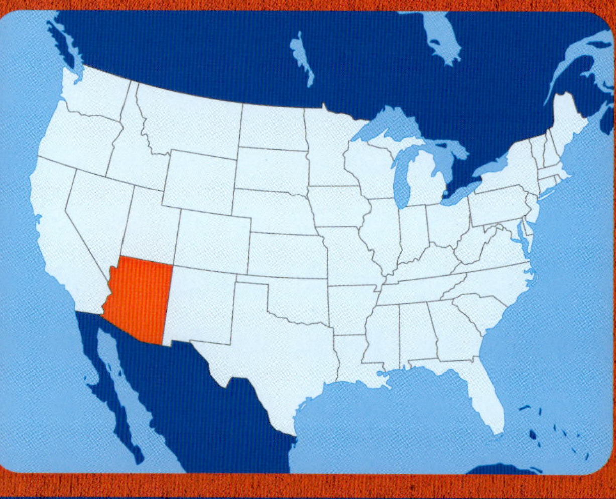

Hoover Dam

Petrified Forest National Park

Arizona: The Grand Canyon State
Utah
Nevada
Lake Powell
Lake Mead
Four Corners Monument
Havasu Falls
Hoover Dam
Colorado River
Grand Canyon
National Park
Flagstaff
Meteor Crater
California
Petrified Forest
National Park
Colorado River
Phoenix
New Mexico
Mesa
Yuma
Gila River
Chandler
Gila River
SONORAN DESERT
Saguaro
National Park
Tucson
MEXICO
Saguaro
National Park
Gulf of California
N
W
E
S

Glossary

elevation
the height above sea level

fossils
the very old, preserved remains of animals or plants

heritage
practices and characteristics that are passed down from one generation to the next

humid
describing air that has a lot of moisture

irrigate
to bring water to land for farming

manufacturing
the process of making goods to sell

meteorite
a rock from space that hits Earth's surface

Online Resources

To learn more about Arizona, visit our free resource websites below.

Visit **abdocorelibrary.com** or scan this QR code for free Common Core resources for teachers and students, including vetted activities, multimedia, and booklinks, for deeper subject comprehension.

Visit **abdobooklinks.com** or scan this QR code for free additional online weblinks for further learning. These links are routinely monitored and updated to provide the most current information available.

Learn More

London, Martha. *Grand Canyon*. Abdo, 2021.

Tieck, Sarah. *Arizona*. Abdo, 2020.

Walker, Cameron. *National Monuments of the USA*. Wide Eyed Editions, 2023.

Index

About the Author

Ib Larsen is a writer and editorial assistant living in Saint Paul, Minnesota.